How Artists See
WORK
Farm Factory Office Home

Colleen Carroll

ABBEVILLE KIDS

A DIVISION OF ABBEVILLE PUBLISHING GROUP

New York London

"Painters understand nature and love her and teach us to see her."

—Vincent van Gogh

For my "brothers," Chuck, Andrew, and David.

I'd like to thank the many people who helped make this book happen, especially Jackie Decter, Ed Decter, Colleen Mohyde, Carolyn Straughan and the Ithaca College Art History Department faculty and staff, and as always, my husband, Mitch Semel.

— Colleen Carroll

Jacket front: Patrick Desjarlait, *Maple Sugar Time,* 1946 (see also pages 32 and 33).
Jacket back, clockwise from upper left: Jacob Lawrence, *Carpenters,* 1977 (see also pages 16 and 17); Maggi Hambling, *Dorothy Mary Crowfoot Hodgkin,* 1985 (see also pages 26 and 27); The Limbourg Brothers, *July, Wheat Harvest with Château of Poitiers,* 1413–16 (see also pages 10 and 11).

Editor: Jacqueline Decter
Designer: Jordana Abrams
Art Director: Patricia Fabricant
Production Editor: Meredith Wolf
Production Manager: Lou Bilka

First edition
10 9 8 7 6 5
ISBN 978-0-7892-0672-5

Library of Congress Cataloging-in-Publication Data
Carroll, Colleen.
Work : farm, factory, office, home / Colleen Carroll.
p. cm. — (How artists see, ISSN 1083-821X)
Includes bibliographical references.
Summary: Examines how people have been depicted working on farms, in factories and offices, and at home in works of art from different times and places.
ISBN 0-7892-0185-2
1. Work in art—Juvenile literature. 2. Art—Juvenile literature. [1. Work in art. 2. Art appreciation.] I. Title. II. Series: Carroll, Colleen. How artists see.
N8219.L2C37 1997
704.9′4331—dc21 97-20745

For bulk and premium sales and for text adoption procedures, write to Customer Service Manager, Abbeville Press, 137 Varick Street, New York, NY 10013, or call 1-800-ARTBOOK.
Visit Abbeville Press online at www.abbeville.com.

CONTENTS

FARM 4

FACTORY 12

OFFICE 20

HOME 28

Note to Parents and Teachers 36

Artists' Biographies 38

Suggestions for Further Reading 43

Where to See the Artists' Work 45

Credits 48

FARM

THE GLEANERS

by Jean-François Millet

At this very moment millions of people are at work, doing all kinds of exciting and important jobs. Doctors are working in hospitals, astronauts are working in space, teachers are working in classrooms, and merchants are working in shops, to name just a few. In this book you'll discover how artists portray people at work: in offices and at home, in factories and on farms. Some of the pictures may even remind you of work you or members of your family do.

One of the oldest forms of work is farming. For thousands of years people have worked the land as a means of survival and to earn a living. In this picture, three women labor in a recently harvested field, picking up the last bits of grain that remain. Although their task is not complicated, it is a physically demanding one. How has the artist shown you the strength of these women?

THE FLOWER CARRIER

by Diego Rivera

Today most of the world's farmers make a living by selling what they produce. In this vividly colored painting, a man waits on his hands and knees while a woman secures a basket of flowers to his back with a yellow cloth. The woman is careful to wrap the fabric in the right place. What might happen if the basket were not properly balanced? Where do you think the man is bringing this glorious basket of flowers?

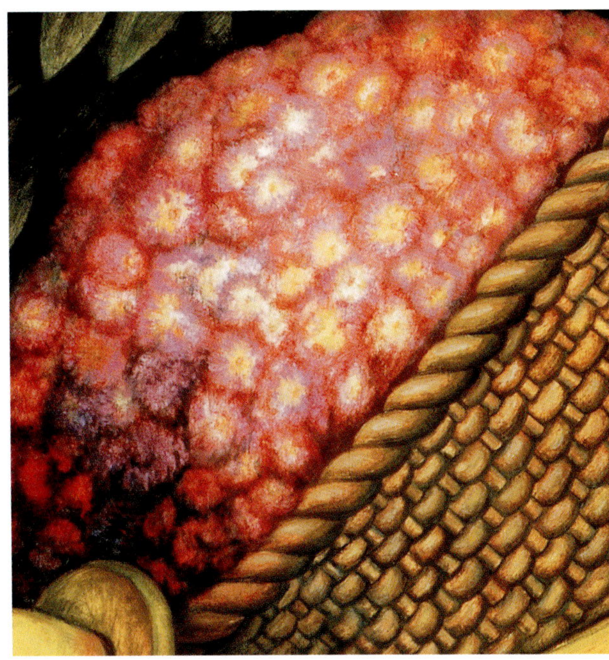

Even though this picture was painted on a piece of smooth canvas, the artist creates the illusion of many different textures, such as the woven cane of the basket and the fluffy flowers. What other textures can you find? If you had to carry this basket, how do you think the cane would feel against your back? How much do you think it weighs?

FARM

HARVESTERS

by Pieter Brueghel the Elder

Here is another picture of farmers harvesting crops on a late summer day. The artist shows the scene from above, as if you were looking down on it from the top of a tall tree. This "birds-eye" view allows you to see the entire farming community at once. As you look down on the scene, you'll notice many different things are happening at one time. Some people are working, such as the men cutting thick walls of grain at the left of the picture, while others

are resting, like the man stretched out for a mid-afternoon nap. What are the others doing?

This artist is known for his close attention to detail, such as the tiny black birds flying over the crops and the bundles of grain lined up in neat rows on the ground. What do you think the triangular structures are supposed to be? In most of this artist's paintings you can even find "a picture within a picture." Look closely at the background. How many separate scenes can you find?

Cancri.
Leonis.
mensis.
Julij.
dies

FARM

JULY, WHEAT HARVEST WITH CHATEAU OF POITIERS

by the Limbourg Brothers

Like the picture you just saw, this page from a medieval calendar also shows some of the typical chores farmers would do in the summer. In the center you see two men reaping grain, while two others shear sheep along a narrow stream. All four workers wear hats, probably to protect their heads from the blazing summer sun. In what other ways do the artists show the heat of this July day?

These laborers probably lived in the quarters to the right of the triangular castle. How do you think they got to and from the fields? The castle is elaborately decorated with flags and towers. Such fine attention to detail makes the picture look realistic. Even the astrological figures in the calendar above the scene are drawn with great care. What other tiny details can you find?

THE GREAT CONSTRUCTORS

by Fernand Léger

Factories, workshops, and construction sites are places of activity, creativity, and lots of hard work. In this picture four men are in the process of erecting a building. They

maneuver among the huge steel girders with grace and skill, almost like high-wire acrobats at the circus. Although construction work can be dangerous and difficult, the men seem completely at ease perched on

these narrow beams and ladders. If this were your job, how do you think it would feel to work so high up in the sky? How tall do you think the building will be when it's finished? For this picture the artist used black, white, and the three primary colors: red, yellow, and blue. Yellow clouds float in the bright blue sky like unfurled flags, and red bars of steel run across and out of the picture as the building grows taller. Why do you think the artist chose these colors? What do you think he is trying to tell you about this type of work?

FORGING THE SHAFT: A WELDING HEAT

John F. Weir

Don't get too close to the furnace, because it is hot! In this picture a group of men work together to guide an enormous iron shaft into a foundry fire. Even with the support of the huge chain, the eight-man crew strains to move the shaft. On the right side of the picture four men are also hard at work. What do you think they are doing?

To help you understand what it was like to work here, the artist used warm colors, such as yellow, red, and orange. The fire's blazing yellow is so bright it illuminates most of the dark space. Where else do you see the fire's yellow light?

CARPENTERS

by Jacob Lawrence

In this busy carpentry workshop, three men go about the business of measuring, drilling, and sawing the wood that will become beautiful handmade objects. How many different kinds of tools can you find? The carpenter on the right leans over his worktable and rests his large hands on a piece of lumber. Why do you think the artist made his hands so big? What do you think he is crafting?

To capture the dynamic energy of this workshop, the artist used bright, bold colors and diagonal lines that run in many different directions. Trace your finger along all the diagonal lines that you see. At how many points do these lines intersect? Close your eyes and imagine the noises you might hear in this room. What do they sound like to you?

CITY BUILDING

Thomas Hart Benton

Even though this picture looks small here, in person it's really quite big—over seven feet tall in fact. This mural, which is a picture painted on a wall, shows the many types of work it takes to build a city. In the lower right-hand corner, you see a man hunched over a set of blueprints. Perhaps he is an architect or an engineer. What other tasks do you see being performed?

The artist creates a feeling of activity by showing the people in a variety of positions. Like dancers, their bodies curve, bend, and stretch as they go about their jobs. Bright colors also capture the energy of the workers and direct your eye from person to person. Starting in the middle of the sky, move your finger to each part where you see the same intense shade of blue. The blue areas are like a road map, telling your eye where to look next. What other colors and shapes guide your eye around the picture?

THE COTTON EXCHANGE AT NEW ORLEANS, OR PORTRAITS IN AN OFFICE

by Edgar Degas

Office work can be loud and chaotic or quiet and solitary. The office in this picture hums with the energy of buying and selling. Throughout the room, businessmen engage in various tasks. Some interact, such as the two men inspecting cotton samples on a long, black table, and some go about their work alone. The spectacled gentleman at the bottom of the picture handles a hunk of cotton, checking its quality up close. One man reads a newspaper, while others just seem to be waiting. What do you think they're waiting for?

This picture is sometimes called *Portraits in an Office.* As you can see, the artist included many people in this composition and paid close attention to the faces of nearly each individual, even some in the background. With one finger, draw an imaginary frame around the head of each man, as if he were the subject of a portrait. Which man do you think was the most important to the artist? Why?

OFFICE AT NIGHT

by Edward Hopper

Sometimes artists get inspiration by looking at the works of other artists whom they admire. The artist who made this picture was familiar with *The Cotton Exchange,* a painting you have already seen. If you look closely, you'll notice a wooden

office chair next to the open door, just like the one in the earlier picture. Now take a few moments to compare both works. In what other ways are they similar? How are they different?

SAINT JEROME IN HIS STUDY

by Albrecht Dürer

Offices can also be places of quiet thought, as you can see in this engraving of Saint Jerome. The saint's study has some of the things you might find in any office, such as a desk, scissors, and books. But it is also like no other study you'll ever see. Born from the artist's fertile imagination, the room is full of things that seem to come out of a fairy tale, such as the sleeping lion at the bottom of the picture. What other unusual things do you see? Why do you think the artist created such a fanciful setting?

Even though this picture is black and white, it's easy to imagine golden sunlight shining through the windows. The animals bask in its warm glow as they snooze, and pools of sunshine dapple the hardwood floor. Where else does the light fall? Look at all the pictures in the book. Which one shows light in a similar way?

DOROTHY MARY CROWFOOT HODGKIN

Maggi Hambling

In this picture the Nobel Prize–winning scientist Mary Hodgkin works at her desk with intense concentration, as you can see by her serious facial expression and forward posture. If you were to tiptoe into her office, do you think she'd notice you? To capture her personality, the artist has included many objects that represent her scholarly pursuits, such as papers, books, files, and a model of a complex molecule.

If you look carefully at the picture, you will notice something unusual: the artist gave her subject four hands instead of two! What is each hand doing? Why do you think the artist chose to show this important and intelligent woman in such a way?

HOME

THE KITCHEN MAID

by Jan Vermeer

As long as there have been houses, there has been housework. What types of chores do you do around the house? In this picture, a kitchen maid is pouring milk into a bowl from an earthenware jug. Perhaps she is adding the milk to a delicious batter that will become bread or cake. The beautiful table is set with a variety of simple foods. What kinds of food do you see? What meal do you think the maid is preparing?

At first glance, this kitchen may seem pretty drab, even a bit boring. But take a second look, and you'll begin to see how the artist used light to transform this plain room into a place full of beauty and dignity. Even the bare, white wall behind the servant seems to glow. Sunlight from the window floods into the tiny space, bringing the room to life with warmth and color. Point to all the places you see the sunlight.

THE FLOOR SCRAPERS

by Gustave Caillebotte

Some types of housework require strength, stamina, and a whole lot of patience. In this picture three men are scraping old varnish from a hardwood floor. The tools of their trade are scattered about, and spiral wood shavings have piled up on the raw wood. The two workers on the right reach forward with their scraping tools. What motion will they need to do to scrape the varnish from the floor? Imagine you are working in this room, and make a scraping motion with your arms.

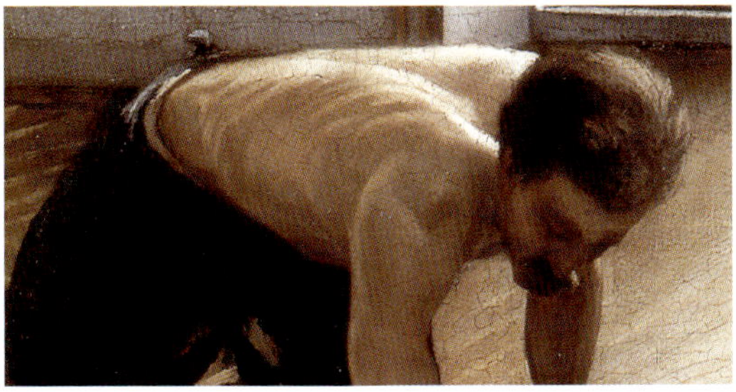

Light from the window shines on the workers' skin, highlighting their muscular backs and arms. Why do you think they've taken off their shirts?

As the workers remove the varnish, a pattern of light and dark brown stripes appears on the floor. These lines lead your eye from the front of the room all the way to the back wall. In what other parts of the room do lines create patterns?

HOME

MAPLE SUGAR TIME

by Patrick Desjarlait

In this picture five people carry out five different jobs that go into making maple syrup. Can you figure out what they are? The people fill up nearly the entire space of the picture, much like the figures in *The Flower Carrier.* In what other ways are the pictures alike?

Fires blaze beneath the iron kettles that hold the boiling sap and cast a warm light over the scene. The people take on the glow of the fire's light and stand out against the shadows of the trees. Even though the many shades of red and yellow give the picture a feeling of warmth, the people wear heavy coats. What does this detail tell you about the time of year and the setting of the picture?

THE QUILTING BEE

by Grandma Moses

There is an old expression that goes like this: "Many hands make light work." What do you think it means? In this lively scene, people from a community have gathered for a work-play party. The main activity is happening at the back of the room, where eight women are putting the finishing touches on a patchwork quilt. After the work is done, the fun can begin, starting with the feast being prepared to the left of the quilters. What other types of work and play can you find?

Although the people appear very stiff, like paper dolls, the picture has the feeling of movement and bustling activity. Nearly every person you see is engaged in some sort of task. If you were a guest at this party, what do you think you would be doing?

You've probably wondered or asked yourself what you want to be when you grow up. A pilot? A veterinarian? An artist? As you have seen throughout this book, there are many kinds of work and nearly as many ways for artists to show people working. Now that you know how some artists see work, try creating your own picture or sculpture of the work that you'd like to do someday.

NOTE TO PARENTS AND TEACHERS

As an elementary school teacher I had the opportunity to show my students many examples of great art. I was always amazed by their enthusiastic responses to the colors, shapes, subjects, and fascinating stories of the artists' lives. It wasn't uncommon for us to spend an entire class period looking at and talking about just one work of art. By asking challenging questions, I prompted the children to examine and think very carefully about the art, and then quite naturally they would begin to ask all sorts of interesting questions of their own. These experiences inspired me to write this book and the other volumes in the *How Artists See* series.

How Artists See is designed to teach children about the world by looking at art, and about art by looking at the world through the eyes of great artists. The books encourage children to look critically, answer—and ask—thought-provoking questions, and form an appreciation and understanding of an artist's vision. Each book is devoted to a single subject so that children can see how different artists have approached and treated the same theme and begin to understand the importance of individual style.

Because I believe that children learn most successfully in an atmosphere of exploration and discovery, I've included questions that encourage them to formulate ideas and responses for themselves. And because people's reactions to art are based on their own personal aesthetic, most of the questions are open-ended and have more than one answer. If you're reading aloud to your children or students, give them ample time to look at each work and form their own opinions; it certainly is not necessary to read the whole book in one sitting. Like a good book or movie, art can be enjoyed over and over again, each time with the possibility of revealing something that wasn't seen before.

You may notice that dates and other historical information are not included in the main text. I purposely omitted this information in order to focus on the art and those aspects of the world it illustrates. For children who want to learn more about the artists whose works appear in the book, short biographies are provided at the end, along with suggestions for further reading and a list of museums where you can see additional works by each artist.

After reading *How Artists See Work,* children can do a wide variety of related activities to extend and reinforce all that they've learned. In addition to the simple activities I've suggested throughout the main text, they can do volunteer work in their community or spend a day at a parent's workplace to experience what it's like "on the job." Since the examples shown here are just a tiny fraction of the great works of art that feature work as their subject, children can go on a scavenger hunt through museums and the many art books in your local library to find other images of work.

I hope that you and your children or students will enjoy reading and rereading this book and, by looking at many styles of art, discover how artists share with us their unique ways of seeing and depicting our world.

ARTISTS' BIOGRAPHIES

(in order of appearance)

If you'd like to know more about the artists in this book, here's some information to get you started:

JEAN-FRANÇOIS MILLET (1814–1875), *pp. 4–5*

As one of fourteen children growing up in a French peasant family, Jean-François Millet (pronounced *mee-YAY*) couldn't have imagined he would become famous for painting pictures of the farmers and field workers he knew from his childhood. He believed that pictures of nature were just as important as portraits or historical scenes, and he is best known for his realistic paintings of farmers and strong peasant women toiling in the fields. During Millet's lifetime many people didn't understand why an artist would want to portray peasants as strong, dignified, and heroic, and his art was often criticized. But it had a strong influence on the work of a young, then unknown artist—Vincent van Gogh.

DIEGO RIVERA (1886–1957), *pp. 6–7*

The Mexican artist Diego Rivera (pronounced *ree-VARE-uh*) was born in Guanajuato, Mexico, along with a twin brother who died a year later. When Diego was still a boy, his family moved to Mexico City, where he studied at the art academy and apprenticed with a wood carver. In his early twenties he traveled to Europe and met many important artists who had a great influence on his artistic style. After he returned to Mexico, he began doing the work he is now famous for: huge murals that depict the history and culture of the Mexican people. Rivera and his wife, Frida Kahlo (an important painter in her own right), were involved in many political causes, and he often included their political beliefs in his work. One of his lifelong goals was to create a national Mexican style of painting, and he sometimes used Pre-Colombian Aztec and Mayan forms and symbols to convey the spirit of Mexico.

PIETER BRUEGHEL THE ELDER (C. 1525–1569), *pp. 8–9*

In 1551 Pieter Brueghel the Elder (pronounced *BROY-gell*) was registered in Antwerp as a "master painter." He left Antwerp in 1551 for Italy, where he saw many works of the Italian Renaissance and made many sketches and studies of the beautiful Italian countryside. From 1555 until his death he lived and worked in Antwerp and Brussels, painting pictures of peasants in everyday situations. Known for his great attention to detail, Brueghel often showed many different activities taking place at the same time in a single painting. Today this Flemish artist is considered to be the most important and gifted Northern European painter of his time.

THE LIMBOURG BROTHERS (DIED 1416), *pp. 10–11*

Pol, Hermann, and Jeannequin Limbourg (pronounced *lam-BOOR*), were born in Holland, but lived and worked most of their lives in France. There is little information about their lives, but it is known that they came from an artistic family (their father was a wood sculptor; their uncle, an artist). In 1408 the brothers began working for Jean, Duc de Berry, brother of the French king. The Duc de Berry was a great patron, or supporter, of the arts, and he kept the brothers busy painting two illuminated manuscripts of the type known as "books of hours." Their masterpiece, called the *Très Riches Heures* (very rich hours), contains beautiful scenes depicting the months of the year. These illuminations were considered modern for the time because they portrayed people in natural settings, used vibrant colors, and included fine details. Mysteriously, all three brothers died in 1416, probably killed by the same plague that took the life of the Duc de Berry. They were all in their twenties.

FERNAND LÉGER (1881–1955), *pp. 12–13*

As a young man Fernand Léger (pronounced *lay-ZHAY*) studied to be an architect, but then switched his attentions to painting. Early in the twentieth century he met the artists Pablo Picasso and Georges Braque, who had created a style of painting known as Cubism. Léger's early paintings show the influence of Cubism, in which the subject seems to be broken into many shapes and is seen from many angles at once. But soon he began to develop his own personal style. He believed that art should reflect the new mechanical age, and the work of his "new realism" period includes images of cylinders, cones, smokestacks, machines, and robots. His mature style is known for his pictures of cartoonlike people set against flat, brightly colored backgrounds, and the themes of his many series include circus performers, divers, cyclists, outings in the countryside, and construction workers. This versatile artist was also a printmaker, set designer, and muralist; he even produced stained-glass windows for churches and public buildings.

JOHN F. WEIR (1841–1926), *pp. 14–15*

In nineteenth-century Europe and the United States, technology and industry were advancing by leaps and bounds. The American artist John Ferguson Weir chronicled this time in American history in his very realistic paintings of factory work. As a boy he studied art with his father, the historical painter Robert W. Weir, and continued his schooling in Europe. After he returned to the United States he became the first director of the Yale School of Fine Art. In his famous painting *The Gun Foundry,* as well as in the one included here, Weir was able to capture the excitement and heat of foundry work by using vivid colors set against a dark background.

JACOB LAWRENCE (BORN 1917), *pp. 16–17*

"My paintings express my life and experience." The artist who spoke those words, Jacob Lawrence, was born in Atlantic City, New Jersey, and later moved with his family to Pennsylvania. After his parents separated, Lawrence and his siblings were first placed in foster homes but were eventually reunited with their mother in the Harlem section of New York City. Shortly thereafter he enrolled in an after-school art class and decided to become a painter. In 1940 he began his masterpiece series, The Migration of the Negro. Its sixty painted panels and text written by the artist tells the epic story of the great migration (1916–30) of African Americans, including his parents, who left the rural South to work in the northern industrial centers of the United States. This series made Lawrence an "overnight success." Lawrence's artwork is noted for its simple, flat shapes, bold colors, and social themes. After teaching art for many years at the University of Washington, Jacob Lawrence retired in 1983. He still lives and makes art in Seattle.

THOMAS HART BENTON (1889–1975), *pp. 18–19*

This opinionated artist from Missouri was part of a small group of artists known as American Scene painters. In the 1930s many American painters were making abstract art, consisting of only line, shape, and color, not realistic, recognizable subjects. But Benton believed that American painting should portray the American landscape and its people. Whether painting a farm scene or a subway, Benton used rounded forms and curving lines to express the dynamic spirit of America as he saw it. The people in Benton's paintings are strong, muscular, and graceful, like those in the work of one of his favorite artists, the Renaissance master Michelangelo. Benton was also a skilled writer and teacher of art.

EDGAR DEGAS (1834–1917), *pp. 20–21*

Born into a wealthy French family, Edgar Degas (pronounced *day-GAH*) is best known for painting pictures of ballet dancers, horse races, and people doing everyday activities. He was part of a group of artists known as the Impressionists, who used color and light in new ways. Most of them worked outside in the natural light, but Degas usually worked in his studio. The other artists were interested in how the sun looked at different times of day, but not Degas. He preferred to show how light appears indoors, especially the dramatic lighting of the theater. Degas is also known for showing how people move; his works capture everything from the graceful movements of a ballerina to the ordinary movement of a lady combing her hair. He lived to be eighty-three years old, and his hundreds of drawings, pastels, and oil paintings can be seen in museums all over the world.

EDWARD HOPPER (1882–1967), *pp. 22–23*

Empty city streets, light-filled rooms, old houses, and brick buildings are some of the subjects that American artist Edward Hopper painted during his long career. He painted in a realistic way, choosing to show the world as it really looks, at a time when many other artists were moving away from this style. Light was very important to Hopper. Many of his paintings show how light can create moods and feelings.

ALBRECHT DÜRER (1471–1528), *pp. 24–25*

As a boy, the German painter, watercolorist, and printmaker Albrecht Dürer (pronounced *DER-er*) was an apprentice in the workshop of a book illustrator. There he learned to draw and make prints, including woodcuts, which are pictures carved into a block of wood that is then inked and pressed onto paper. Although Dürer was a talented painter, it was his prints, especially his woodcuts and engravings, that made him famous, because they were sold all over Europe. He was a master at showing detail, light, shadow, and energy in his work. He also wrote books on his scientific and artistic ideas. Many people consider him one of history's most gifted artists.

MAGGI HAMBLING (BORN 1945), *pp. 26–27*

The English artist Maggi Hambling didn't realize she had artistic talent until she was a teenager. As part of a school exam, she was required to draw a picture. Her teacher noticed Hambling's drawing ability and encouraged her to attend art school. Hambling feels that drawing is "the most direct and intimate thing an artist can do," and she fills sketchbook after sketchbook with her studies and drawings. As a painter she is known for her quick brushwork and brilliant use of color. Some of her most common subjects are sunrises and sunsets, bullfights, and people.

JAN VERMEER (1632–1675), *pp. 28–29*

Of all the great artists throughout history, Jan Vermeer is perhaps the most mysterious, because so little is known about his life. He spent his entire life in Delft, Holland, where he worked as a tavern keeper and was, like his father, an art dealer. Of the thirty-odd paintings that have been attributed to him, all but a few depict one or several people inside a small room going about the simple tasks of everyday life. Because most of Vermeer's paintings are so well executed and similar in style, some historians believe that his early work may have been destroyed in an explosion that occurred in Delft during his lifetime. Vermeer died at the age of forty-three, and for more than two hundred years after his death his work remained all but unknown, enabling the Vermeer forger Hans van Meegeren to perpetrate the greatest art hoax of the twentieth century.

GUSTAVE CAILLEBOTTE (1848–1894), *pp. 30–31*

Many people buy art in the hope that their collection will be worth a lot of money in time. But the French architect and amateur painter Gustave Caillebotte (pronounced *kye-yuh-BOHT*) collected only artwork that appealed to him. As luck would have it, in 1874 he met three young artists who were making paintings with an unusual and altogether original look. The artists were Claude Monet, Edgar Degas (see *The Cotton Exchange*), and Auguste Renoir. That same year Caillebotte organized the infamous art exhibit that gave these artists the name now known the world over: Impressionists. Until recently Caillebotte's own painting was all but ignored, but a 1994 traveling exhibition introduced his art to thousands of people. His most famous painting, *Paris Street: Rainy Day,* beautifully captures the elegance of that city in the nineteenth century. Upon his death Caillebotte left his large collection of Impressionist paintings to the French government; they now hang in the Louvre Museum in Paris.

PATRICK DESJARLAIT (1921–1972), *pp. 32–33*

When Native American artist Patrick Desjarlait (pronounced *day-zhar-LAY*) was a child, he liked to paint portraits of people he knew. They called him "little boy with a pencil." As a young man, Desjarlait spent a year at the Chippewa Reservation and later said that he felt "compelled to tell the story of my people through my paintings." Born into the Ojibway tribe, Desjarlait was awarded a scholarship to attend Arizona State College in Phoenix; after graduating, he joined the United States Navy. He admired the art of Pablo Picasso and Diego Rivera (see *The Flower Carrier*) and incorporated aspects of their work into his own. Because his paintings capture and celebrate the richness of his Native American heritage, Desjarlait is considered by many to be one of the most important Native American artists of the twentieth century.

ANNA MARY ROBERTSON "GRANDMA" MOSES (1860–1961), *pp. 34–35*

Imagine beginning a new career at age seventy-eight! That's exactly how old Anna Mary Robertson Moses was when she decided to become a professional painter. The artist known as "Grandma" Moses was born in 1860 in upstate New York. After her marriage in 1887, she kept very busy working the family farm and raising her five children. In her spare time she made and sold potato chips! She was in her early forties when she made her very first painting in the folksy style that would make her famous. Because she had no formal training in painting, she is considered a "primitive" artist. Most of her pictures are filled with people going about their daily lives in beautiful rural settings. In 1940 a New York City newspaper dubbed her "Grandma" Moses, and the name stuck. Anna "Grandma" Moses painted up until a few months before her death in 1961. She was 101 years old and left behind more than 1,500 paintings.

SUGGESTIONS FOR FURTHER READING

The following children's titles are excellent sources for learning more about the artists presented in this book:

FOR EARLY READERS (AGES 4–7)

Anholt, Laurence. *Degas and the Little Dancer: A Story About Edgar Degas.* Hauppauge, New York: Barron's, 1996.
This sweet—and true—story of the little girl who modeled for Degas's bronze sculpture *The Little Dancer* incorporates facts about the life and art of the famous French artist.

Venezia, Mike. *Edward Hopper.* Getting to Know the World's Greatest Artists series. Chicago: Children's Press, 1990.
This easy-to-read biography combines color reproductions and humorous illustrations to capture the personality and talent of the famous twentieth-century American artist. Included in this series are *Diego Rivera* and *Pieter Bruegel,* also by Mike Venezia.

Winter, Jeanette, and Jonah Winter. *Diego.* New York: Knopf, 1991.
A Reading Rainbow book selection, this delightful story presents the life of the Mexican artist Diego Rivera from his early childhood into adulthood. Bilingual text is in Spanish and English.

FOR INTERMEDIATE READERS (AGES 8–10)

Holland, Gina. *Diego Rivera.* Illustrated by Gary Rees. First Biographies series. Austin, Texas: Raintree/Steck Vaughn, 1997.
This biography recounts the life of the Mexican painter who worked to create a distinctively Mexican artistic style.

Howard, Nancy Shroyer. *Jacob Lawrence: American Scenes, American Struggles.* Worcester, Mass.: Davis Publications, 1996.
Engaging text, colorful illustrations, and fun activities combine to give children a thorough introduction to the life and art of Jacob Lawrence.

Lawrence, Jacob. *The Great Migration: An American Story.* New York: Harpercrest, 1993.
In his own words and pictures, the American artist tells the story of the thousands of African Americans who left the South in search of work and a better life in the industrial North.

Littlesugar, Amy. *Marie in Fourth Position: The Story of Degas' "The Little Dancer."* Illustrated by Ian Schoenherr. New York: Philomel Books, 1996.
The charming story of the poor French girl who modeled for Degas's famous bronze sculpture *The Little Dancer.*

O'Neal, Zibby. *Grandma Moses: Painter of Rural America.* Illustrated by Donna Ruff. New York: Viking, 1987.
The early life of the American folk painter is captured in this biography.

Raboff, Ernest. *Albrecht Dürer.* Art for Children series. New York: HarperCollins, 1988.
This informative book describes the life, times, and style of this German Renaissance artist.

Sterchx, Pierre. *Brueghel: A Gift for Telling Stories.* Art for Children series. New York: Chelsea House, 1994.
The life and art of the master Flemish painter Pieter Brueghel the Elder is told in this book, complete with many full-color reproductions of his work.

FOR ADVANCED READERS (AGES 11+)

Biracree, Tom, and Nancy Tomplins. *Grandma Moses.* American Women of Achievement Series. New York: Chelsea House, 1989.
The life and art of America's most famous folk artist is told in this biography for children.

Cockcroft, James. *Diego Rivera.* Hispanics of Achievement Series. New York: Chelsea House, 1991.
This biography introduces children to the life, art, and politics of the Mexican artist best known for his public murals.

Desjarlait, Patrick, and Neva Williams. *Patrick Desjarlait: Conversations with a Native American Artist.* Minneapolis: Runestone Press, Lerner Learning Group Publishers, 1995.
Narrated by the artist, this books tells the fascinating and true story of Desjarlait's life as a Native American and career as an artist.

Hickok, Beth Moses. *Remembering Grandma Moses.* Bennington, Vt.: Images from the Past Publications, 1994.
In this book the artist's daughter-in-law fondly recollects the life of her famous relative.

Loumaye, Jacqueline. *Degas: The Painted Gesture.* Illustrated by Nadine Massart. Art for Children series. New York: Chelsea House, 1994.
The distinguished French artist "narrates" this clever, engaging biography.

Mühlberger, Richard. *What Makes a Bruegel a Bruegel.* New York: The Metropolitan Museum of Art and Viking, 1993.
The life and work of the Flemish painter is explored in an examination that shows children how to recognize the artist's unique style. Also in this series is *What Makes a Degas a Degas* by the same author.

Skira-Venturi, Rosabianca. *A Weekend with Degas.* New York: Rizzoli, 1992.
Imagine spending a weekend with the famous French Impressionist. This informative and clever book takes you back in time as the painter tells of his life and work. Also in this series is *A Weekend with Diego Rivera* by Barbara Braun.

WHERE TO SEE THE ARTISTS' WORK

THOMAS HART BENTON

- Albrecht-Kemper Museum of Art, St. Joseph, Missouri
- Bakersfield Museum of Art, California
- Barbara and Steven Grossman Gallery, School of the Museum of Fine Arts, Boston
- Hunter Museum of Art, Chattanooga, Tennessee
- Minnesota Museum of Art, St. Paul
- National Museum of American Art, Smithsonian Institution, Washington, D.C.
- The New School for Social Research, New York
- Sheldon Swope Museum, Terre Haute, Indiana
- http://www.arches.uga.edu/~smead/Benton.html

PIETER BRUEGHEL

- British Museum, London
- Kunsthistorisches Museum, Vienna
- Louvre, Paris
- The Metropolitan Museum of Art, New York
- Musées Royaux des Beaux-Arts, Brussels
- Museo Nazionale, Naples
- Museum of Fine Arts, Budapest
- National Gallery, Prague
- Prado, Madrid
- Timken Museum of Art, San Diego
- http://sunsite.unc.edu/cjackson/bruegel1

GUSTAVE CAILLEBOTTE

- The Art Institute of Chicago
- Kimbell Art Museum, Fort Worth, Texas
- Milwaukee Art Center
- Minneapolis Institute of Arts
- Musée d'Orsay, Paris
- Musée du Petit Palais, Geneva
- Museum of Fine Arts, Boston
- Museum of Fine Arts, Houston
- National Gallery of Art, Washington, D.C.
- Virginia Museum of Fine Arts, Richmond
- http://watt.emf.net/wm/paint/auth/caillebotte

EDGAR DEGAS

- The Art Institute of Chicago
- Burrell Collection, Glasgow, Scotland
- Cleveland Museum of Art
- Denver Art Museum
- Solomon R. Guggenheim Museum, New York
- The Metropolitan Museum of Art, New York
- The Minneapolis Institute of Arts
- Musée des Beaux-Arts, Pau, France
- Musée d'Orsay, Paris
- Museum of Fine Arts, Boston
- National Gallery, London
- Philadelphia Museum of Art
- The Phillips Collection, Washington, D.C.
- Pushkin Museum, Moscow
- Norton Simon Art Foundation, Pasadena

- Thyssen-Bornemisza Collection, Lugano, Switzerland
- http://sunsite.unc.edu/cjackson/degas
- http://www.navigo.com/wm/paint/auth/degas

PATRICK DESJARLAIT

- Heard Museum, Phoenix, Arizona
- Minnesota History Museum, St. Paul
- Minnesota Museum of American Art, St. Paul
- Philbrook Museum of Art, Tulsa, Oklahoma
- http://indy4.fdl.cc.mn.us/~isk/art/art_minn.html

ALBRECHT DÜRER

- Crocker Art Museum, Sacramento, California
- The Metropolitan Museum of Art, New York
- Museum of Fine Arts, Boston
- National Gallery of Art, Washington, D. C.
- Pinakothek, Munich
- St. Louis Art Museum
- http://sunsite.unc.edu/cjackson/durer

MAGGI HAMBLING

- British Museum, London
- Foundation du Musée de la Main, Lausanne, Switzerland
- National Gallery, London
- National Portrait Gallery, London
- Tate Gallery, London
- Yale Center for British Arts, Yale University, New Haven, Connecticut

EDWARD HOPPER

- Delaware Art Museum, Wilmington
- Hopper House/Edward Hopper Preservation Foundation, Nyack, New York
- Montclair Art Museum, Montclair, New Jersey
- Portland Museum of Art, Maine
- Walker Art Center, Minneapolis
- Whitney Museum of American Art, New York
- http://sunsite.unc.edu/cjackson/hopper

JACOB LAWRENCE

- Bellevue Art Museum, Washington
- High Museum of Art, Atlanta
- Museum of Modern Art, New York
- National Academy of Design, New York
- National Museum of American Art, Smithsonian Institution, Washington, D.C.
- The Phillips Collection, Washington, D.C.
- Studio Museum in Harlem, New York
- Frederick R. Weisman Art Museum, University of Minnesota, Minneapolis
- http://hudson.acad.umn.edu/Lawrence/WAMjacobtest.html

FERNAND LÉGER

- The Art Institute of Chicago
- The Solomon R. Guggenheim Museum, New York
- Kröller-Müller Museum, Otterlo, Netherlands
- Milwaukee Art Center, Wisconsin
- Musée Fernand Léger, Biot, France
- Museum of Modern Art, New York
- National Museum of Modern Art, Paris
- Philadelphia Museum of Art
- Tate Gallery, London
- http://www.grandwailea.com/art/leger/leger.html

THE LIMBOURG BROTHERS AND ILLUMINATED MANUSCRIPTS

- The Cloisters, New York
- J. Paul Getty Museum, Los Angeles
- Louvre, Paris
- The Metropolitan Museum of Art, New York
- Pierpont Morgan Library, New York
- Musée Condé, Chantilly, France
- National Gallery of Art, Washington, D.C.
- http://sunsite.unc.edu/wm/rh

JEAN-FRANÇOIS MILLET

- Arnot Art Museum, Elmira, New York
- Louvre, Paris
- Musée d'Orsay, Paris
- Museum of Fine Arts, Boston
- Philadelphia Museum of Art
- Toledo Museum of Art, Ohio
- http://netspot.city.unisa.edu.au/wm/paint/auth/millet

ANNA MARY ROBERTSON MOSES

- Bennington Museum, Vermont
- The Metropolitan Museum of Art, New York
- Midwest Museum of American Art, Elkhart, Indiana
- National Museum of Women in the Arts, Washington, D.C.
- The Phillips Collection, Washington, D.C.
- Shelburne Museum, Shelburne, Vermont
- http://www.neinfo.net/New_England/Vermont/Bennington/Attractions/Benninton_Museum/Grandma_Moses.htp

DIEGO RIVERA

- Detroit Institute of Arts, Michigan
- Honolulu Academy of Arts
- Los Angeles County Museum of Art
- McNay Art Museum, San Antonio, Texas
- Museum of Modern Art, New York
- Museo Nacional de Arte, INBA, Mexico City
- Philadelphia Museum of Art
- Phoenix Art Museum
- Diego Rivera Museum, Guanajuato, Mexico
- San Francisco Museum of Art
- Spanish Museum of Contemporary Arts, Madrid
- http://www.diegorivera.com/diego_home_eng.html

JAN VERMEER

- Frick Collection, New York
- Gemäldegalerie, Berlin
- Louvre, Paris
- The Metropolitan Museum of Art, New York
- National Gallery, Dublin
- National Gallery, London
- National Gallery of Scotland, Edinburgh
- National Gallery of Art, Washington, D.C.
- Rijksmuseum, Amsterdam
- Städelsches Kunstinstitut, Frankfurt
- http://www.cacr.caltech.edu/~roy/vermeer/

JOHN F. WEIR

- Mattatuck Museum, Waterbury, Connecticut
- The Metropolitan Museum of Art, New York
- Putnam County Historical Society, Cold Spring, New York

CREDITS *(listed in order of appearance)*

Jean-François Millet (1814–1875). *The Gleaners,* 1857. Oil on canvas, 32⅝ × 43⅝ in. (83 × 111 cm). Musée d'Orsay, Paris. © Hubert Josse/ Abbeville Press, New York. Diego Rivera (1886–1957). *The Flower Carrier,* 1935. Oil and tempera on masonite, 48 × 47¾ in. (121.9 × 121.3 cm). San Francisco Museum of Modern Art; Albert M. Bender Collection, Gift of Albert M. Bender in memory of Caroline Walter. Pieter Brueghel (the Elder) (c. 1525–1569). *Harvesters,* 1565. Oil on panel, 46½ × 63¼ in. (118.1 × 160.6 cm). The Metropolitan Museum of Art, New York; Rogers Fund, 1919. The Limbourg Brothers (all b. after 1385–all d. by 1416). *July, Wheat Harvest with Château of Poitiers,* 1413–16. Illumination from the *Très Riches Heures du Duc de Berry.* Musée Conde, Chantilly, France. © Art Resource. Fernand Léger (1881–1955). *The Great Constructors.* In *Contrastes,* 1959. Pochoir, 22 × 26 in. (55.9 × 66.1 cm). Private collection. © Bob Ruschak/Abbeville Press, New York. John Ferguson Weir (1841–1926). *Forging the Shaft,* 1874–1877. Oil on canvas, 52 × 73¼ in. (132.1 × 186.1 cm). The Metropolitan Museum of Art; Gift of Lyman G. Bloomingdale, 1901. Jacob Lawrence (1917–). *Carpenters,* 1977. Lithograph, 18 × 22 in. (45.7 × 55.9 cm). John Hechinger Collection, Landover, Maryland. © Joel Berger. Thomas Hart Benton (1889–1975). *City Building,* 1930. Egg tempera and distemper, 92 × 117 in. (233.7 × 297.2 cm). Equitable Insurance Co., New York. Edgar Degas (1834–1917). *The Cotton Exchange at New Orleans, or Portraits in an Office,* 1873. Oil on canvas, 29⅛ × 36¼ in. (73 × 92 cm). Musée des Beaux Arts, Pau, France. © Reunion des Musées Nationaux, Paris. Edward Hopper (1882–1967). *Office at Night,* 1940. Oil on canvas, 22¼ × 25⅛ in. (56.5 × 63.8 cm). Walker Art Center, Minneapolis, Minnesota; Gift of the T. B. Walker Foundation, Gilbert M. Walker Fund, 1948. Albrecht Dürer (1471–1528). *Saint Jerome in His Study,* 1514. Engraving, Musée du Petit Palais, Paris. © Art Resource, New York. Maggi Hambling (1945–). *Dorothy Mary Crowfoot Hodgkin,* 1985. Oil on canvas, 36¾ × 30 in. (93.2 × 76 cm). By courtesy of the National Portrait Gallery, London. Jan Vermeer (1632–1675). *The Kitchen Maid,* c. 1658. Oil on canvas, 17⅞ × 16⅛ in. (45.4 × 40.9 cm). Rijksmuseum, Amsterdam. Gustave Caillebotte (1848–1894). *The Floor Scrapers,* 1875. Oil on canvas, 40⅛ × 57⅜ in. (102 × 146 cm). Musée d'Orsay, Paris. © Hubert Josse/ Abbeville Press, New York. Patrick Desjarlait (1931–1972). *Maple Sugar Time,* 1946. Watercolor, 15¼ × 20¼ in. (38.7 × 20.3 cm). Philbrook Museum of Art, Tulsa, Oklahoma. Grandma Moses (1860–1961). *The Quilting Bee,* 1950. Oil on pressed wood, 20 × 24 in. (50.8 × 61 cm). Private collection. © 1982 Grandma Moses Properties Company, New York.